Lincolnshire
COUNTY COUNCIL

discover libraries

This book should be returned on or before the last date shown below.

To renew or order library books please telephone 01522 782010
or visit www.lincolnshire.gov.uk
You will require a Personal Identif...
Ask ...

First published 2012

The History Press
The Mill, Brimscombe Port
Stroud, Gloucestershire, GL5 2QG
www.thehistorypress.co.uk

British Library Cataloguing in Publication Data.
A catalogue record for this book is available from the British Library.

ISBN 978 0 7524 6798 6

Typesetting and origination by The History Press
Printed in Great Britain
Manufacturing managed by Jellyfish Print Solutions Ltd.

Coat of Arms

The new coat of arms for the unified Brighton and Hove is a combination of their previous armorial bearings.

*

The two dolphins are taken from the Brighton arms, where they had long been in use. Their origins are somewhat clouded by the mists of time, but may either reflect the town's coastal situation or their usage on the arms of several leading local families.

*

The ship run ashore on a shingle beach commemorates the French attacks on Hove in the early sixteenth century.

*

The surrounding six martlets on a blue background represent the county of Sussex.

*

The motto, INTER UNDAS ET COLLES FLOREMUS, means 'Between Downs and Sea We Flourish'.

Contents

Pronunciation

Pronounced /ˈbraɪtən/

'Brighton' came into common usage at the start of the nineteenth century, and is a shortening of the older Anglo-Saxon term 'Brighthelmstone'. This may have been derived from the combination of 'Brighthelm', a South Saxon bishop, and 'tun', a homestead. There were many variations on this name, and in the Domesday Book the term 'Bristelmestune' was used.

Hove

Pronounced /ˈhoʊv/

'Hove' most likely originated from a medieval word for anchorage.

Grid Reference

Peace Statue, Hove Lawns

Ordnance Survey Grid Reference: TQ 299041

Street Names

The city has a great many road names reflecting its past regal and imperial links, Queens Road and Kings Road being the most obvious. Apart from these, surprisingly little creativity has gone into naming the streets of Brighton and Hove. The Brow, The Cliff, The Curve and The Down are typically uninventive, although perhaps descriptive names.

The least imaginative award, however, goes to those planners who dreamt up First Avenue, Second Avenue, Third Avenue and Fourth Avenue, when constructing the 'West Brighton' Estate, in Hove.

The numerical theme was also used for major road junctions in the city, although at least Fiveways and Seven Dials describe the roads leading into them. Other junctions include Preston Circus and The Vogue Gyratory, a roundabout so big that the people who live on it have their own pub and a petrol station.

So dull are the names that some locals have taken to adding their own improvements.

Villages and Neighbourhoods

In Brighton and Hove but not Brighton and Hove:

Rottingdean

Saltdean

Ovingdean

Woodingdean

Stanmer Village

Patcham

Preston

West Blatchington

Hangleton

Mile Oak

Portslade

Some Neighbourhoods in Brighton and Hove:

North Laines

The (posh) Lanes

Kemptown

Brunswick

Goldsmid

Moulsecoomb

Whitehawk

Withdean

Hanover

Queens Park

Distances From

Place	Miles	Km
Amsterdam, Holland	241	389
Bali, Indonesia	7,783	12,525
Cape Town, South Africa	5,963	9,597
Dieppe, France	82	132
Edinburgh, Scotland	376	604
Frankfurt am Main, Germany	391	629
Granada, Spain	958	1541
Hong Kong	6,006	9,666
Ibiza	829	1,335
Jerusalem	2,220	3,573
Kingston, Jamaica	4,683	7,536
London	47	76
Mumbai, India	4,471	7,196
New York, USA	3,475	5,593
Olympia, Greece	1,401	2,255
Perth, Australia	8,992	14,472
Quebec, Canada	3,118	5,018
Rio de Janeiro, Brazil	5,729	9,219
San Francisco, USA	5,395	8,683
Tokyo, Japan	5,981	9,626
Ulan Bator, Mongolia	4,364	7,023
Vancouver, Canada	4,748	7,641
Warsaw, Poland	910	1,465
Xuzhou, China	5,434	8,745
Yucatan, Mexico	4,984	8,021
Zanzibar, Tanzania	4,578	7,368

Where Are You From?

A Random Survey of People on the Beach, Christmas Day, 2011

Tina	North London
James	Manchester
Mafuene	Cape Town
Hannah (three and a half years old)	My Mummy and Daddy
Steve	Banbury
Jane	Southampton
Alicia	Barcelona
Mellow	Hove
Yara	Rio de Janeiro
Donia	London
Ben	Brighton
Father Christmas (so he claimed)	Lapland

Twinned With?

Despite the absence of any formal twins, it could be argued that the city is informally twinned with London. Whilst a large number of seasiders endure the daily lottery that is the commute to the capital, even greater hordes have been coming in the other direction in the pursuit of leisure.

Londoners have dreamt up all manner of events just to escape London for the south coast, involving a variety of modes of transport. These include:

The Pioneer Motorcycle Run

The Historic Commercial Vehicle Rally

The Mini Rally

The MG Regency Run

The Land Rover Run

The Veteran Car Run

The Classic Car Run

The Ace Café Reunion

The Jaguar Run

The Brighton Breeze Split Screen VW Run

The British Heart Foundation London to Brighton Cycle Ride

One woman even walked (or should that be rolled) to Brighton on top of a large ball!

Other Brightons and Hoves

In Adelaide, South Australia, the districts of Brighton and Hove are adjacent to each other on the coast. Apart from this example, international Brightons and Hoves are widely separated, with Brightons all over the world but only rarely in Europe, whilst other Hoves are to be found only in northern Europe.

Brightons

Brighton, Malaysia

Brighton, Bolivia

Brighton, Jamaica

Brighton, Barbados

Brighton, Trinidad

Brighton, Guyana

Brighton, New Zealand

There are also four in Canada, five in Australia, and over half the states in the USA have Brightons, some more than one.

Hoves

Hove, Germany

Hove, Belgium

Hove, Denmark

Hove, Norway

Hove, Faroe Islands

Historical Timeline

Celtic Iron Age hill forts at Hollingbury, Ditchling Beacon and Devil's Dyke.

Bristelmestune recorded in Domesday Book.

Chalk rock deposited during the Cretaceous era.

Stone Age camp on Whitehawk Hill.

Saxons start settling in Sussex.

145-65,000,000 BC   3-4000 BC   600 BC   500   1086

200,000 BC   2000 BC   150 AD   800   1312

Neanderthals hunted mammoths on Tertiary Sands behind the Asda Marina car park.

Saxon burials near Seven Dials.

Roman villa south of Preston Park.

King Edward II gi permission to hav a market and an annual fair aroun Bartholomew's Da

Bronze Age settlements at Coldean and Patcham; Woodhenge at Mile Oak; amber cup buried in Hove tumulus.

Charles II hides in Brighton before escaping to France.

The London to Brighton train line opens.

Greater Brighton and Greater Hove increase in size due to boundary changes.

ch
tes raid
ingdean,
ing fire
e church
th the
gers in it.

Dr Richard Russell publishes paper on medicinal benefits of taking sea water.

Brighton and Hove granted city status by Queen Elizabeth II.

377   1651   1750   1841   1928   2000

1514   1703/05   1783   1850   1997

Medieval
Brighton and
Hove burnt to
he ground by
French raiders.

The Prince of Wales visits Brighton for the first time.

Brighton and Hove joined as a unitary authority.

Storms destroy the Lower Town on the beach.

Queen Victoria sells the Royal Pavilion to Brighton Corporation.

Freak Natural Events

The city's coastal location is an attraction to locals and visitors alike. On rare occasions, however, this puts it in the meteorological frontline, as storms, hurricanes and even a tidal wave have battered its beaches.

1665 – Violent storm washes away shops and cottages of the Lower Town of Brighton.

1703 – Daniel Defoe describes another 'dreadful tempest' that destroys several boats and their crews.

1705 – 'Every habitation under the cliff was utterly demolished' by a storm. The Lower Town ceases to exist. Hove loses its South Well.

1824/1833/1836 – Series of storms and lightning strikes damage the Chain Pier.

1896 – A storm finally destroys the Chain Pier.

1929 – Tidal wave 12ft high washes over the beaches – miraculously there was only one fatality.

1987 – The infamous 'no cause for alarm' hurricane causes a large amount of structural damage and uproots many trees inland.

Just Another Day

The Market Diner is
in full swing serving
the legendary
Gutbuster fry up to
the post pub and
club crowd.

The nightshift at Sussex
County Hospital comes
off duty.

Last of the bleary eyed
clubbers meander home
to an infernally loud dawn
chorus as the city's avian
population wakes up.

0300   0600   0800

0000   0530   0719   1010

The nightclubs
get busy as some
pubs close.

Brighton to Victoria train
sets off – another day of
commuter joy beckons.

Refuse collectors and bus
drivers start getting the city
ready for another day.

Students get the first
off-peak train to Faln
less money and a
longer lie in.

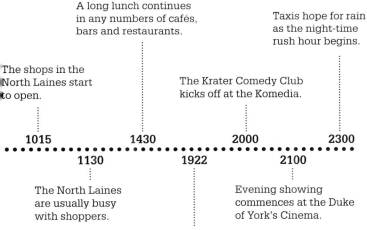

A long lunch continues in any numbers of cafés, bars and restaurants.

Taxis hope for rain as the night-time rush hour begins.

The shops in the North Laines start to open.

The Krater Comedy Club kicks off at the Komedia.

1015

1430

2000

2300

1130

1922

2100

The North Laines are usually busy with shoppers.

Evening showing commences at the Duke of York's Cinema.

The 18.17 out of Victoria hopefully arrives at Hove; this being 'rush' hour, it has stopped at eight different stations on the way.

How Many ...

Babies were born in the city in 2009?– 3,274

There were 1,653 girls and 1,621 boys

Journeys commenced or finished at Brighton Station in 2010? – 13,741,582

In this year Brighton Station was the ninth busiest in the country outside of London

Journeys the eight railway stations in the city were used for in 2010? – Over 19 million

Tourists visit the city every year? – 8 million

6.5 million are day trippers. They spend over £400 million a year

Meetings per year take place for horse racing fans at the Brighton Racecourse? – 20

Days (and nights) dogs race at the Hove Greyhound Stadium every year? – 250

Bus journeys were made in the city in 2010? – More than 41 million

MÁIRE MCSORLEY

Demographics

	Brighton & Hove	England & Wales
Population	258,800	52,041,916
Percentages		
Female	51.6	51.3
Male	48.4	48.7
Over 16 and never married	43.4	30
Over 16 and married	30.5	43.6
One person households	44.45	30.02
Married households	23.9	36.55
Cohabiting households	11.55	8.28
Single parent households	8.59	9.52
Christian	59.1	71.75
Jedi	2.6	0.7
No religion	27.02	14.81
Households with no car	36.54	26.79
Households with two or more cars	19.64	29.44

Máire McSorley

Number Crunching

82.5 – Life expectancy at birth for girls.

77.1 – Life expectancy at birth for boys.

3,360 – Number of listed buildings and structures in Brighton and Hove.

22,500 – The capacity of the Amex Stadium, home of Brighton and Hove Albion.

40,000 – The number of motorcycles ridden into the city for the Ace Café Reunion.

27,000 – The number of participants in the London to Brighton cycle ride.

Nearly 1,400 – Premises licensed to sell alcohol.

250,000 – The number of people who crowded onto the beach and Kings Road for Fatboy Slim's Big Beach Boutique II in 2002.

8 – The number of different railway stations from which you can catch a train within the city's boundaries.

£2,634,059 – The cost to build the Brighton to London railway line, opened in 1841.

Over 370 billion – The number of pebbles on the beach.

A City with Two Piers

Opened in 1866, the West Pier was 1,115ft in length. Closed in 1975 and neglected by a range of organisations that could have saved it, bad weather and two arson attacks in the space of two months have reduced it to the ghostly shell now visible.

The Grade II listed Palace Pier (renamed by the owners as the Brighton Pier in 2000) opened in 1899, at a then record cost of £27,000. It is 1,719ft long, and is currently up for sale.

The City in Literature

'We shall have no peace at Longbourn if Lydia does not go to Brighton. Let her go, then. Colonel Forster is a sensible man, and will keep her out of any real mischief; and she is luckily too poor to be an object of prey to anybody. At Brighton she will be of less importance even as a common flirt than she has been here.'

Jane Austen, *Pride and Prejudice*, 1813

'But have we any leisure for a description of Brighton? – for Brighton, a clean Naples with genteel lazzaroni – for Brighton, that always looks brisk, gay, and gaudy, like a harlequin's jacket.'

William Makepeace Thackeray, *Vanity Fair*, 1848

'The Castle of this ogress and child-queller was in a steep by-street at Brighton; where the soil was more than usually chalky, flinty, and sterile, and the houses were more than usually brittle and thin; where the small front-gardens had the unaccountable property of producing nothing but marigolds, whatever was sown in them; and where snails were constantly discovered holding on to the street doors, and other public places they were not expected to ornament, with the tenacity of cupping-glasses.'

Charles Dickens, *Dombey and Son*, 1848

'I've never changed. It's like those sticks of rock. Bite one all the way down, you'll still read Brighton. That's human nature.'

Graham Greene, *Brighton Rock*, 1938

Máire McSorley

What They Said About Brighton and Hove

'A country so truly desolate that if one wanted to hang oneself for desperation at being obliged to live there, it would be difficult to find a tree upon which to fasten a rope.'

Samuel Johnson reflecting on the Downs surrounding the city

'It is so situated that a coach, which leaves it early in the morning, reaches London by noon: and starting to go back in two hours and a half afterwards, reaches Brighton not very late at night. Great parcels of stockjobbers stay at Brighton with the women and children. They skip backward and forward on the coaches and actually carry on stock-jobbing in Change Alley, while residing in Brighton.'

William Cobbett commenting on the first commuters

'I hate going out in Brighton now. It's different in London. People respect you more there.'

Katie Price

'Brighton is a town that looks like it is helping the police with their enquiries.'

Keith Waterhouse

IMMEDIATELY
TO THE SOUTH OF THIS
BUILDING STOOD THE HOUSE
OCCUPIED BY
HESTER AND HENRY THRALE
WHERE SAMUEL JOHNSON
AND FANNY BURNEY
WERE FREQUENT
VISITORS
ERECTED BY THE REGENCY SOCIETY

Famous for ...

Seagulls

The beach

Laid-back people

Nightlife

Brighton Festival

Pride

The Pavilion

Brighton Rock

Infamous for ...

Bank holiday traffic

Stag nights

Hen nights

West Street at night

Heroin deaths

Trunk murders

Bank holiday punch ups in the 1960s

Seagulls

Inside and Outside – St Bartholomew's Church

Some of the Activities Licensed by the Council

Alcohol (sale of)

Births, marriages and deaths

Body piercing

Dog breeding

Electrolysis

Exotic, wild or dangerous animals

Gambling premises

Lotteries

Riding establishments

Semi-permanent skin-colouring

Sex establishments

Stage hypnotism

Street trading (including hot chestnut selling)

Tattooing

Taxis

What the Papers Said

The Times, 30 August 1792

On Monday Mrs Fitzherbert gave a grand dinner to his Royal Highness the Prince of Wales and a party of his friends, at her house in Marlborough Row, Brighton. In the evening his Royal Highness with the company honoured the Subscription Ball at the Castle with their presence, which was numerously attended, 290 persons being present. The Ball did not break up till four o'clock on Tuesday morning.

The Brighton Gazette, 16 September 1841

The Brighton Terminus is a beautiful structure, and with the iron sheds in the rear, will not suffer from comparison with any railway terminus in existence. The offices and waiting rooms are most commodious, and are furnished with every convenience for passengers. Gas fittings for the whole terminus have been put up by Brighton and Hove General Gas Company.

Brighton Herald, 10 November 1928

An expression which we used last week concerning Mrs Burden, the unsuccessful candidate in the Lewes Road Ward election, seems capable of misconstruction. We referred to her as having 'Left-Wing sympathies'. Apparently this has been interpreted as suggesting that Mrs Burden is a communist. We are therefore bound to state emphatically that no such suggestion was intended by our Note. Mrs Burden is no communist. She is a keen and ardent representative of the working classes who has done excellent public service.

The Times, 22 July 1929

COAST TOWNS SWEPT BY WAVE

Preceded by sharp gusts of wind and a period of calm, a line of foam rushed towards the beach, while pleasure boats rushed for safety. Almost before the crowds realized what was happening torrential rains poured down and the wave rushed far up the beach, carrying away chairs and bather's clothes.

The Times **18 April 1933**

BRIGHTON CLOCK TOWER

Brighton Council will at its next meeting discuss a proposal
for the demolition of the clock tower which is well known
to all the people going from the railway to the seafront. One
prominent member of the council said: 'The clock tower
is both hideous and an obstruction. It must make way for
modern Brighton. There will be no proposal from us for its
removal and re-erection elsewhere. We suggest its demolition
and the use of the debris for road metal.'

Rebellious Brighton and Hove

1555 – Deryk Carver, brewer of Black Lion Street, was tried for reading the Bible in English. He was sentenced to death, and taken to Lewes, where he was burnt in a barrel of pitch. As the fire was lit, his last words were: 'And because I will not deny here God's Gospel, and be obedient to man's laws, I am condemned to die.'

1926 – The Battle of Lewes Road was a clash outside the tram depot during the General Strike. Several thousand strikers and their supporters were brutally dispersed by a large police contingent, supported by a force of Sir Harry Preston's mounted Special Volunteers.

1980s – The Battle of Farm Rd was a confrontation between the mechanics who plied their trade in the mews workshops, and the traffic wardens who wanted to ticket their customers' cars parked on the road outside. The local constabulary arrived in time to prevent harsh words becoming harsher deeds.

1996/1997 – Supporters of Brighton and Hove Albion felt betrayed by the club's Board of Directors, who had sold the Goldstone Ground without organising an alternative venue for the team. Several pitch invasions were followed by a campaign that saw Albion fans marching through London and lobbying in Lancashire. At home games mass protests were the norm, and on several occasions the Chief Executive was made to feel so unwelcome that he left rapidly. Novel protest tactics were used, including boycotts and 'Fans United' games, where supporters from all over the country came and showed solidarity. A new board was convened at the end of 1997, but it would be another fourteen years before the Albion would play at their own stadium.

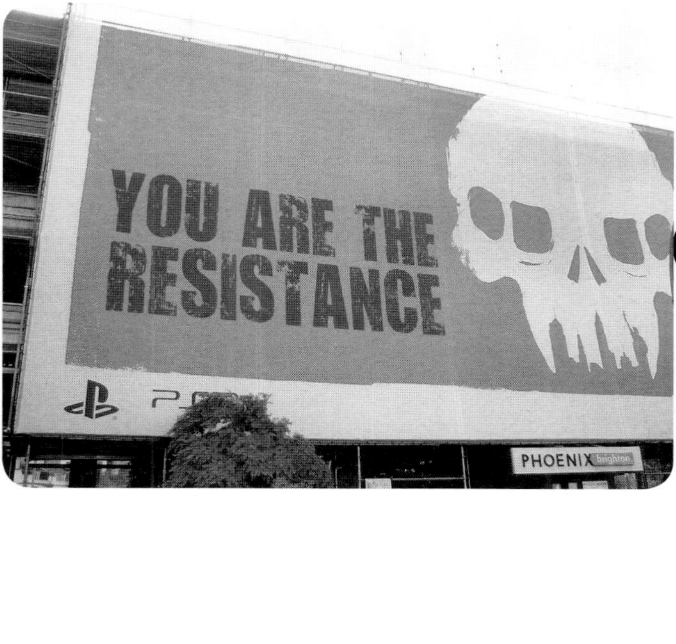
YOU ARE THE
RESISTANCE
PHOENIX brighton

A City with Two Universities

The city has two universities, Brighton and Sussex, employing over 4,000 people and hosting over 35,000 students. Together they contribute hundreds of millions of pounds to the local economy.

University of Brighton – Designated as a university in 1992, the institution traces its roots to the foundation of the Brighton School of Art in 1859. 23,000 students are based at five sites; Falmer, Moulsecoomb and Grand Parade in Brighton, and Eastbourne and Hastings.

Alumni include DJ Jo Whiley and Whitbread winning artist Rachel Whiteread.

University of Sussex – The university was established by Royal Charter in 1961. The campus was originally designed by Sir Basil Spence, and its 12,000 students enjoy the use of many listed buildings, including the Grade I listed Falmer House.

Among those who have studied at Sussex are musician Billy Idol and Nigel Planer of *The Young Ones*.

Regency Architecture

The city's most famous architectural inheritance is its Regency buildings, not least because so many have survived. This is particularly so on the seafront between Hove and Kemptown where, apart from occasional intrusions of modernity, the Regency façade is near continuous, having successfully endured storms, sea air, Hitler's bombers, and perhaps most dangerously, the attentions of developers.

The Regency Society, set up in 1945 in response to the plans of post-war modernisers, has played a large part in protecting this now valued heritage.

As they were in many other fields of more positive developments, the city's forefathers were also unfortunately ahead of the curve when it came to modernising the built environment. Former Mayor Sir Herbert Carden famously declared in the inter-war years that the Regency estate should be demolished and replaced with more modern structures, this despite the fact that he lived on Marine Parade himself. It is the city's good fortune that on this occasion he did not get his way.

Victorian Architecture

Away from the seafront the Victorians have left their architectural mark, particularly in the form of commercial and institutional buildings.

Brighton Railway Station – This Grade II listed gateway to the city for many millions of visitors, past and present, was opened in 1840. The most spectacular feature is the double spanned glass and iron roof, which dates from 1883. Thankfully plans to modernise the station came to nothing, and the roof was lovingly restored in 2000.

The British Engineerium – In West Blatchington, this was originally constructed as a water pumping station by the Brighton, Hove and Preston Constant Water Service Company in 1866, to meet the increasing demand for clean water in the growing urban area. Scheduled for demolition in 1971, steam enthusiast Jonathan Minns successfully campaigned for the listing of the site, and subsequently restored the complex, opening it as a museum in 1976. Following financial difficulties the collection was sold to local businessman Mike Holland in 2006, and has been under renovation ever since. It may reopen in 2012, although concerns over the welfare of a resident badger colony have apparently delayed work.

Art Deco Architecture

Although not many Art Deco buildings survive, the ones that do are gems.

Embassy Court – Completed in 1936, this stands out in the midst of its Regency neighbours. Following years of post-war neglect and decay it was listed in 1984, a necessary first step on the long road to its eventual restoration in 2006, at a cost of £4.6 million. Once again it now sits proudly as a rare successful example of modernism on the seafront.

The Saltdean Lido – This has enjoyed an equally chequered history. Opened in 1938, it shut down the following year for the duration of the war and for some years afterwards. Listed in 1987, it suffered closure again between 1995 and 1998. Plans submitted by the current leaseholder in 2010 to build flats on the site have led to the formation of the Save Saltdean Lido campaign, which has succeeded in upgrading the Lido's listed status to Grade II in 2011. The future remains uncertain for this Art Deco gem.

Modern Architecture: The Good, the Bad and the Ugly

The Jubilee Library – Opened in 2005, at a cost of £14 million. Its glass south wall is constantly altering in appearance, reflecting activity in Jubilee Square and the fluctuating sky. One million visits a year and only 50 per cent of the carbon emissions of most similar sized structures – even the rainwater is collected to flush the loos. Definitely the good.

The Brighton Centre – Opened in 1977 at a cost of £9 million, it has been much maligned for its bland and unimaginative appearance, a trait probably not mitigated by being adjacent to the equally uninspiring Kingswest Centre. Some would suggest that without the centre the city couldn't host party political conferences or mega-groups like Deep Purple. Many more would probably be prepared to make that sacrifice. Bad!

New England House – Opened in 1964, this has claims to be the world's first purpose-built high rise industrial business centre. Many locals would ask if it was also the last. It does however provide much needed affordable space for small local businesses, and there are plans to turn it into a hub for creative and digital start-ups. It has been described as being an example of Brutalist Architecture. Despite its utility, most people describe it as just plain ugly.

Iconic Image

Museums

It's raining, and the kids probably want to spend your money on the pier. Here are some more cultural, and mostly free, alternatives.

Booth Museum of Natural History

Brighton Fishing Museum

Brighton History Centre

Brighton Museum and Art Gallery

Brighton Toy and Model Museum

British Engineerium (opening in 2012, maybe)

Grange Museum

Hove Museum and Art Gallery

Old Police Cells Museum

Preston Manor

The Royal Pavilion

... Okay kids, we'll go to the pier now!

The Dome

The Dome, perhaps more than any other building in the city, encapsulates the history of Brighton and Hove. Today the Dome Complex, including the Corn Exchange and the Pavilion Theatre, is the home of the Brighton Festival and a centre of cultural life.

1806 – Built as stables for the Prince of Wales

1850 – Purchased from Queen Victoria as part of the Pavilion Estate

1856 – Let out as a cavalry barracks

1867 – Converted into a concert hall at a cost of £10,000

1915 – Used as a hospital for Indian soldiers wounded on the Western Front

1920s – Hosted boxing matches promoted by Sir Harry Preston

1935 – Refurbished at a cost of £50,000

1972 – Pink Floyd come to The Dome to premiere their new album 'Dark Side of the Moon'

1974 – Abba win the Eurovision Song Contest at the Dome, singing Waterloo

1998 – Annual turnover of £1 million

2002 – Reopens after refurbishment at a cost of £30 million

2008 – Annual turnover of nearly £10 million

INDIA'S FIGHTING MEN, PAVILION GROUNDS, BRIGHTON

V & H

South Downs National Park

At the start of April 2011 the South Downs National Park became Britain's newest national park. Covering an area of 1,645 square kilometres between Winchester and Eastbourne, it is the third largest – and most populous – of such parks. It is also the most popular, receiving some 39 million visitor days a year (the figure for the Lake District being around 8 million visits).

Over 40 per cent of Brighton and Hove lies within its boundaries, mainly to the north and the east of the city. Much of this land is owned by the council, purchased in the first half of the twentieth century to protect the city's water supply from development.

To protect the rich biodiversity of the chalk grasslands (and to reduce the £25,000 bill for grass cutting) the council has brought in a flock of sheep to graze right up to the urban fringe. The sheep are monitored by a team of eighty volunteer shepherds drawn from the city, who are also known as 'lookerers'.

Parks and Green Spaces

Brighton and Hove has ninety-eight parks and public open spaces in a variety of urban and rural settings, as well as 2,800 allotments and 229 sports pitches, greens and courts.

Six of the parks have attained 'Green Flag' status:

Easthill Park

Hove Park

Kipling Gardens

Preston Park

St Ann's Well Gardens

Stoneham Park

Other popular locations include:

Dyke Road Park

East Brighton Park

The Level

Pavilion Gardens

Queens Park

Stanmer Park

Wild Park

Flora and Fauna

The city is home to the National Elm Collection, which comprises around 30,000 trees. Whilst in the rest of the country their numbers have been decimated by Dutch Elm Disease, the local population has survived due to the isolation provided by the sea and the surrounding downs, and the efforts of the council's Arboricultural Service. The 'Preston Twins', at an estimated 400 years of age, are probably the oldest specimens in the world.

At sunset during the winter months one of the most spectacular sights is the flying display put on by tens of thousands of starlings, as they circle and swoop as if one, over the piers. These 'murmurations' take place nightly before the birds roost under the piers.

Somewhat less popular, but no less iconic, amongst our feathered friends is the European Herring Gull. They can create a lot of mess when looking for food, and leave an even bigger one when it comes out the other end. Notwithstanding their social shortcomings, they are now on the RSPB's endangered 'Red List', and 'The Seagulls' is of course the nickname for Brighton and Hove Albion, whose crest they proudly adorn.

Home of the
National Elm Collection Brighton & Hove

You are entering an Elm Disease Management Area

For information call (01273) 292187

Top Ten Employers

Brighton and Hove Council	9,000
Brighton and Sussex University Hospitals NHS Trust	5,800
American Express	3,500
University of Sussex	2,100
University of Brighton	2,000
Legal and General	1,600
Lloyds TSB	1,500
South Downs Health Care Trust	1,500
EDF Energy	1,200
ASDA	1,150

From Little Acorns ...

At the other end of the corporate scale there are over 19,000 self-employed people in the city.

Outside the top ten employers, there are over 13,400 other businesses in the city.

Most people (97.6 per cent) work for an organisation employing less than 50 people.

One of the most successful retail start-ups to hail from the city was The Body Shop. Now one of the largest cosmetic retail franchises in the world, with 2,400 outlets in over sixty countries, The Body Shop was founded by the late Dame Anita Roddick from a shop front in Kensington Gardens in 1976. Having overcome some disagreements with a neighbouring funeral director regarding the name of the store, she took the chain from strength to strength, and it was eventually taken over by L'Oreal in 2006.

Another retail success, and many would say closer to its founding principles, is Infinity Foods. Founded in 1971, this workers co-operative has always aimed to provide high quality vegetarian produce, and has grown alongside the sizeable local market for natural and organic foods.

Nightlife

The city is famed for its ever evolving nightlife – kids, the first column (below) is where your parents used to dance (probably a worrying thought). Parents, the second list is where your kids now go (an even more worrying thought):

The Zap	Digital
The Escape	Audio
The Concorde	Concorde II
Funky Buddha Lounge	The Tube
The Beach	The Brighton Coalition
The Honey Club	The Honey
Revenge	Revenge
The Event `	Oceana
The Volks	The Volks
The Jazz Rooms `	The Jazz Place
Enigma	The Loft
Arc	Life
Pavilion Tavern	Pavilion Tavern
Sumo	Jam

New kid on the block:

Green Door Store

Gone but not forgotten:

The Pressure Point

The Ocean Rooms

The Gloucester

A City with Two Harbours

The city has two complementary harbours, the leisure oriented Brighton Marina and the more industrial Shoreham Harbour.

Shoreham Harbour

There has been a harbour here since Roman times, although the present configuration dates back to 1760.

Commercial vessels in port in 2010 – 787

Fishing vessels in port in 2010 – 1,123

Brighton Marina:

Opened – 1979

1,600 berths

863 residential properties

Brighton and Hove Firsts

Dating back to early 1882, the city has the oldest continuous public electricity supply in the world.

The Volks Electric Railway carried its first passengers in 1883, and was the first in England to be powered by electricity. Still in operation today, it runs from near the Palace Pier to Black Rock. The short lived 'Daddy Long Legs' electric railway ran on some of this route at the end of the nineteenth century.

In the late nineteenth and early twentieth centuries Brighton Corporation bought up surrounding countryside to protect the urban water supply – creating a green belt long before the Green Belt (London and Home Counties) Act of 1938 became law.

2010 – The voters of Brighton Pavilion constituency elected Caroline Lucas as Britain's first ever Green Party MP.

2011 – The people of Brighton and Hove elect Britain's first Green Party administration to run the city council.

Local Characters

The origins of much of the present-day city can be traced back to three larger than life characters in the first half of the twentieth century:

Sir Herbert Carden is often referred to as the 'maker of modern Brighton'. Elected as a Socialist councillor in the Hanover ward in 1895, he would become the dominant figure in the Brighton Corporation for many years. Through his influence the Corporation acquired most of the surrounding countryside, as well as providing the services and infrastructure that modernity required, such as electricity, telephones and transport. Whilst his role in resolving Brighton's notorious slum housing problems is held in high regard, he was less popular for his proposals to demolish the Regency seafront and the Pavilion.

Harry Cowley, known affectionately as 'The Guv'ner', was a survivor of the trenches on the Western Front, a chimney sweep by trade, and a grass roots activist and organiser by vocation. After the First World War he was at the forefront of efforts to secure work for the unemployed and entitlements for the poor. Both the Open Market and the Upper Gardner Street markets owe their current status to his organisational efforts. He led the fight against Mosley's fascists before the Second World War and against homelessness after it. His name lives on through the Cowley Club on London Road.

At the other end of the political spectrum was **Sir Harry Preston**, councillor and entrepreneur. From his base at the Royal York and Royal Albion Hotels, he was a champion of motorised sport and its associated commercial interests. He convinced the council to tarmac Madeira Drive in order that he could hold the speed trials that continue to this day. He was also a leading proponent (supported by Carden) of the inter-war plan to build a 5-mile long motor race circuit on the downs near Devil's Dyke. He was less popular with the demonstrators who felt the blows landed by his volunteer 'specials' assisting the police during the General Strike.

Máire McSorley

Crime

Piracy

The Sussex coast has a lengthy history of 'nautical' activity that was outside of the law. Whilst the privateers operating out of Shoreham Harbour in the seventeenth century were officially licensed to carry out acts of piracy on French and Spanish vessels, the more localised acts of wrecking and smuggling had no such official sanction.

As early as the fourteenth century, the owners of a Portuguese merchant ship that had gone aground off Hove complained that the local population were far too keen in their efforts to rescue the cargo whilst the crew awaited the next high tide.

Smuggling

Smuggling was something of a cottage industry, so institutionalised that a vicar in Rottingdean was apparently an accomplice. One of his colleagues in Hove had to cancel a service as his pulpit was being used to store chests of tea, and the church itself was full of barrels.

Murder

Perhaps the most notorious crimes were the 'Trunk Murders'. The first of these was in 1831 when John Holloway killed his wife Celia to get out of paying maintenance after they had separated. The unfortunate Celia was dismembered and her torso buried in a trunk. Holloway was convicted and hanged.

More recently there were two, probably unrelated, murders in 1934. The torso of a young pregnant woman was found in a trunk at Brighton Station, and whilst there were suspicions that a local abortionist was involved, no charges were ever brought. In the second case the victim was found in a trunk at the foot of her pimp's bed. He was acquitted at the trial, but later confessed in a newspaper interview in 1976.

Máire McSorley

Brighton and Hove Under Attack

Over the centuries the Sussex coast has faced numerous attacks from the French and the elements. Regular French raids culminated in the attack of 1514 when Brighton and Hove were burnt to the ground. In response the appropriately named Sir John Wallop assembled a fleet and set about the villages of Normandy in a similar fashion.

During the Second World War there were a total of fifty-six air raids, which killed 198 people. The beaches were closed and heavily fortified, defences that were fully justified when the details of the German invasion plan, Operation Sea Lion, became known. The plans showed that Brighton and Hove were to be directly attacked by Hitler's Ninth Army from the sea, and by paratroopers from behind.

During the 1960s the city's beaches became a war zone in a different context, as Mods and Rockers regularly invaded the south coast on Bank Holidays.

Most recently the city has been the focus IRA bombing attacks. The Grand Hotel bombing in 1984 was an attempt to assassinate Margaret Thatcher. She survived but five other people died.

In 1994 another device was attached to a bicycle near the Palace Pier, but this was successfully defused.

Brighton Festival

For three weeks in May the city hosts the Brighton Festival, the largest multi-arts event in England. From its launch in 1967 the event has grown to be the highlight of the city's cultural calendar, and now attracts 300,000 visitors to over 160 events.

The complimentary Brighton Fringe Festival, more 'open-access' in nature, runs at the same time, with 100,000 attending over 600 events. The Fringe City event brings over 40,000 people to New Road for three days of street performances and entertainment.

The Festival commences with the carnival of the Children's Parade, which proceeds from Sydney Street to Madeira Drive, involving 5,000 young people. It closes three weeks later with a large firework display on the seafront.

Pride

The Pride weekend encompasses a range of events, including the loud and colourful parade with floats from Madeira Drive through the streets to Preston Park around Saturday lunchtime, with a party in Preston Park afterwards.

In the past up to 160,000 revellers have been in attendance at the free celebration, although a new ticket purchasing system for Preston Park in 2011 reduced numbers to a perhaps more comfortable level.

There are a number of other events over the weekend, of which the largest is the street party in the St James Street neighbourhood in Kemptown, which attracts over 20,000 visitors over the two days.

Other Festivals

There is almost always something going on in the city. Here are just a few of the other festivals and events held in the city:

Brightona motor cycle event

Brighton Carnival

Brighton Food and Drink Festival

Brighton Kite Festival

Burning the Clocks (Winter Solstice)

Chocolate Festival

Cine-City Film Festival

Great Escape Music Festival

Hove Lions Carnival

Kemptown Carnival

Paddle Round The Pier

Springwatch

White Nights Festival (Clocks go back)

World Naked Bike Ride (Brighton leg)

… as well as far too many local community events to mention.

Artists and Writers in Residence

Steve Bell (cartoonist)

William Black (author)

Julie Burchill (author)

John Constable (painter)

Charles Dickens (author)

James Herbert (author)

Rudyard Kipling (author)

Peter O'Donnell (author)

John Osborne (playwright)

Robert Rankin (author)

Terence Rattigan (playwright)

Philip Reeve (author)

Louise Rennison (author)

J.M.W. Turner (painter)

Keith Waterhouse (author)

Robert Vaughn Williams (composer)

Rex Whistler (painter)

Helen Zahavi (author)

HERE
LIVED
1897 – 1903
RUDYARD KIPLING
1865 – 1936
PLACED HERE BY THE
KIPLING SOCIETY

SIR
TERENCE
RATTIGAN C.B.E.
Playwright
lived here

ERECTED BY THE REGENCY SOCIETY

Performing Artists – Past and Present

Pete Bennett (*Big Brother* winner)

Cate Blanchett (actress)

Captain Sensible (musician)

Nick Cave (musician)

Charlie Chaplin (actor)

Steve Coogan (comedian)

Fatboy Slim (musician)

Nigel Kennedy (musician)

Max Miller (comedian)

Anna Neagle (actress)

Lawrence Olivier (actor)

Rizzle Kicks (musicians)

Flora Robson (actress)

Robert Smith (musician)

Dusty Springfield (musician)

Tommy Trinder (comedian)

Mark Williams (comedian)

On Location – Films Shot in the City

Brighton and Hove were centres for the embryonic British film industry in the late nineteenth century. The oldest surviving 'adult' film in the United Kingdom was made in 1896, in a back garden in Hove, with the warning that it was appropriate for no one but Gentlemen's Smoking Concert audiences!

More recent cinematic offerings from the city include:

Brighton Rock (1947)

Genevieve (1953)

Cast a Dark Shadow (1955)

Oh! What a Lovely War (1969)

On a Clear Day You Can See Forever (1970)

Carry on at Your Convenience (1971)

Tommy (1975)

Quadrophenia (1979)

Mona Lisa (1986)

Dirty Weekend (1993)

Wimbledon (2004)

The Da Vinci Code (2006)

Angus, Thongs and Perfect Snogging (2008)

The Young Victoria (2009)

Brighton Rock (2010)

A City with Over Five Miles of Coastline

The city enjoys over 5 miles of seafront, made up of four differing environments, each with a distinct character:

The Undercliff Walk from the Marina to Rottingdean is a path that follows the coastline beneath the iconic white cliffs, and is largely undeveloped.

The Kemptown beachfront, between the Marina and the Palace Pier, provides a quieter urban setting, and includes the nudist beach. If you're feeling lazy the Volks Electric Railway runs the length of this stretch.

Between the piers is the classical seaside resort, bustling with a matching range of amusements and attractions. After the day-trippers have departed, action switches to the seafront nightclubs.

The Hove seafront is quieter and more restrained, beach huts and lawns having replaced the noisier activities on the other side of the West Pier. The pétanque players can get quite rowdy though, with polite applause and understated approval greeting a successful 'technical fanny'.

Sussex County Cricket Club

Founded in 1839 – the oldest county side in England.

Supporters of Sussex had waited patiently for 113 years before they could celebrate their team finally winning the County Championship in 2003. Then they went and won it again in 2006 and 2007.

During the most successful spell in the club's history they also collected:

The Friends Provident Trophy – 2006

The Pro 40 National League – 2008, 2009

Twenty20 Cup – 2009

Best Batting – 344*, M.W. Goodwin v Somerset at Taunton (2009)

Best Bowling – 10-48, C.H.G. Bland v Kent at Tonbridge (1899)

Best Match Bowling – 17-106, G.R. Cox v Warwickshire at Horsham (1926)

Brighton and Hove Albion FC

The Albion have recently emerged from the most troubled period in their history, which saw their old Goldstone Ground sold, the fans travelling to Gillingham for home matches, and a return to the city in the temporary surroundings of the athletics track at Withdean.

Having won the Division 1 title in style in 2010/2011, the Albion celebrated their promotion to the Championship by moving into the brand new Amex Stadium, rising out of the Downs at Falmer.

1901 – Brighton and Hove Albion founded

1910 – Won the Charity Shield: Albion 1, Aston Villa 0

1920 – Elected into Football League Division 3

1958 – Record Crowd: 36,747 against Fulham

1976/77 – Record League goalscorer: Peter Ward – 32

1979 – Albion promoted to the First Division

1981/82 – Highest ever league position:
(Old) First Division – thirteenth

1983 – FA Cup Finalists and relegated to Second Division

1997 – Last game at the Goldstone Ground

2010/11 – Winners of League One

2011 – Record Signing – £2.5 million: Craig Mackail-Smith

2011 – First season at the Amex Stadium and in
The Championship

Sports Personalities

Gareth Barry (football) – Now playing for Manchester City and England, he started with Brighton and Hove Albion.

Chris Eubank (boxing) – World Middleweight and Super Middleweight Champion – purchased the title of Lord of the Manor of Brighton.

Tommy Farr (boxing) – British Heavyweight Champion who lost narrowly on points to Joe Louis – ran the Royal Standard pub on Queens Road after he retired.

Des Lynam (presenter) – Versatile all-rounder who has commentated and presented for the BBC, ITV and Channel 4. A long time Albion supporter.

Ryan Moore (horse racing) – three times Champion Jockey – winner of The Derby, Oaks, King George, Arc de Triomphe and Breeders Cup Turf.

Steve Ovett (athletics) – World record holder and Olympic Champion – born in Brighton and went to Varndean School.

David Stone (paracycling) – Double gold medal winner at the Beijing Paralympics – graduated from the University of Brighton.

Virginia Wade (tennis) – Last British winner of a Wimbledon singles title – studied physics at the University of Sussex.

Alan Weeks (commentator) – Covered the Winter and most Summer Olympics for the BBC – his career started at the SS (Sports Stadium) Brighton in West Street.

Beach Sports

For those with a desire to do something more active than just erecting a deckchair, here are just some of the beach sports available between the Marina and Hove Lagoon:

Basketball

Beach volleyball

Climbing

Crazy golf

Cycling

Kayaking

Pétanque

Sailing

Skateboarding

Swimming

Ultimate Frisbee

Wind Surfing

The Loneliness of Long Distance Runners

The city has a complementary mix of charitable and commercial distance running events.

The season kicks off in February with the Brighton Half Marathon, now over twenty years old. Since 2004 the event has been organised by the Sussex Beacon, a charitable organisation that provides support for men and women living with HIV/AIDS. Over 8,000 runners cover a course that primarily follows the seafront.

The Brighton Marathon is a more recent addition to the city's sporting calendar and, in its second year in April of 2011, had over 8,000 runners being cheered on through the streets by around 80,000 spectators.

The Brighton 10K road-race is run along the seafront during November. Organised by the Brighton and Hove City Athletics Club, it had 2,500 runners competing in 2010.

Street Art

At the start of the 1990s the most famous piece of graffiti was probably the advice to 'GO ON – PHONE IN SICK', written in 3ft letters on a wall high above the Seven Dials junction, perfectly placed to catch the eyes of drivers stuck in the rush hour traffic queues on their way to work.

More recently the city has seen a wave of officially sanctioned street art on both permanent walls and temporary hoardings, seen as being far more decorative than the previously widespread random taggings.

Money has rapidly followed the growing popularity of some works, to the extent that the iconic 'Kissing Policemen' by Banksy is reputed to be going to America, where it may command as much as a $1 million at auction.

Far more colourful works can be seen all around the city, with Kensington Street in the North Laines being a particularly rich street gallery.

At your Convenience

Older public conveniences around the city have been put to a number of novel uses, including estate agents and cafés. A few are still used for their original purpose.

Things to Do in Brighton and Hove – Checklist

Soak up the bohemian atmosphere of the North Laines. ☐

Watch the starlings performing their aerial ballet over the piers. ☐

Watch people trying to find their friends on the crowded beach after they have gone to the bathroom/bar/café. ☐

Make sure you have taken your bearings before you leave your friends on the beach to go to the bathroom/bar/café. ☐

Get your hiking boots on and walk along part of the South Downs Way. ☐

Watch the morning drift into the afternoon from one of the city's numerous pubs, cafés and restaurants. ☐

Enjoy the sunset from the beach with (or without) a cold bottle of wine. ☐

Witness the opulence of Regency living (if you were the Regent) at the Pavilion. ☐

Enjoy the wide range of cultural entertainments during the Festival. ☐

Dance the night away at one of the many nightclubs. ☐

Visit the Brighton Wheel and test your acrophobia (fear of heights). ☐

Useful Websites

http://www.brighton-hove.gov.uk/index.cfm

http://www.visitbrighton.com/

http://www.brighton-hove-rpml.org.uk/RoyalPavilion/Pages/home.aspx

http://www.brightonfestival.org/

http://brightonfestivalfringe.org.uk/nextyear/

http://www.brightonsource.co.uk/

http://www.dontpaniconline.com/brighton

http://www.gscene.com/index.shtml

http://whatson.brighton.co.uk/

http://www.sussex.ac.uk/

http://www.brighton.ac.uk/

Image Credits

Back flap. Royal Pavilion (Tanay Sharma)

2. Welcome to Brighton and Hove (Tanay Sharma)

3. Brighton and Hove coat of Arms (Brighton and Hove City Council)

7. Bandstand (Tanay Sharma)

9. The Peace Statue (Tanay Sharma)

10. Kemptown beach in winter (David Boyne)

10. Pavilion gardens in bloom (David Boyne)

11. Elm trees on The Level – St Peter's church in the background (Tanay Sharma)

11. Street art on Ditchling Road (Tanay Sharma)

13. Elder Peace (David Boyne)

13. (Se)Vere Road (David Boyne)

15. Rottingdean Windmill (Tanay Sharma)

17. San Francisco (Paul.h)

17. The Alhambra in Granada (Jim Gordon)

19. Table Mountain in Cape Town (Andrew Massin)

19. Copacabana Beach, Rio de Janeiro (Chensiyuan)

21. Vintage Car Rally (David Boyne)

21. Historical Commercial Vehicle Rally (Mark Woolford)

23. The Brighton Wheel (Mark Woolford)

24. Mammoth (Titus 332)

24. Edward II

25. Railway viaduct

25. Queen Victoria

27. Storm front over Kemptown seafront (David Boyne)

27. Church in nearby St Leonards damaged in the 1987 'Hurricane' (Phil Sellens)

28. Kensington Gardens in the late morning (Tanay Sharma)

29. The Brighton Wheel (Mark Woolford)

31. Brighton Racecourse (Tanay Sharma)

31. Clock at Brighton Station (Máire McSorley)

33. Sunset at the Doughnut sculpture on the seafront (Máire McSorley)

35. Reflection in motor-cycle mirror, Marine Parade (David Boyne)

35. Pavilion silhouette (David Boyne)

37. The West Pier (Tanay Sharma)

37. The Palace Pier (Tanay Sharma)

39. William Makepeace Thackeray (Jessie Harrison Whitehurst)

39. Rooftops (Máire McSorley)

41. Samuel Johnson looking suitably cheerful … (Gilbert/J. Linton)

41. … he would have been even more unhappy if he visited West Street today! (David Boyne)

43. Statue of George IV (Tanay Sharma)

45. Statue of Queen Victoria (Tanay Sharma)

46. St Bartholomew's church from the inside (Tanay Sharma)

47. St Bartholomew's church on the outside (Tanay Sharma)

For more information about the photographers whose images have illuminated this book:

Tanay Sharma: https://www.facebook.com/tansharma.photography
Máire McSorley: maire.mcsorley@virginmedia.com or facebook page Máire McSorley – Artist and Photographer.